SECRETS

Since the dawn of civilisation man has been surrounded by mysteries. As man developed he managed to solve many things that at first appeared to have no rational explanation but even now, in this age of super technology, there remain many things that just cannot be explained – or can they? SECRETS OF THE UNKNOWN looks at some of these hitherto inexplicable mysteries, examines the stories that surround them, and attempts to offer rational explanations for their existence.

Some of the strange mysteries looked at in SECRETS OF THE UNKNOWN include: UFOs, GHOSTS AND HAUNTINGS, THE LOCH NESS MONSTER, THE POWER OF THE PYRAMIDS and THE TRIANGLE OF DEATH. You can even test yourself to see whether *you* possess PSYCHIC POWERS . . .

Jacket artwork by Geoff Taylor

Secrets of the Unknown

Gordon Hill

Illustrated by Donald Harley

KNIGHT BOOKS
Hodder and Stoughton

Printed and bound in Great Britain for
Hodder and Stoughton Paperbacks, a
division of Hodder and Stoughton Ltd,
Mill Road, Dunton Green, Sevenoaks,
Kent (Editorial Office: 47 Bedford
Square, London, WCI 3DP) by
Hunt Barnard Printing Ltd,
Aylesbury, Bucks.

ISBN 0 340 24039 3

Contents

Foreword

Man has always been fascinated by the unknown, by strange and mysterious happenings that he cannot explain despite his own extraordinary progress in the realms of science.

Over the years a special vocabulary has developed to describe anything to do with this dark and shadowy world that may exist alongside our own. As you read *Secrets of the Unknown* you will come across some of these words. Here is a list of those you may not know already. You will find that others are explained in the text as you read.

Astrology is the study of the way our behaviour is influenced by the stars and planets. Horoscopes published in newspapers are an example of this science.

Astronomy is the scientific study of the stars and planets.

Coincidence describes a fact or an event which is remarkably related or similar to another one, without there appearing to be a connection.

Divination is the use of magic to try to see into the future. It can also refer to the tracing of underground water by using a hazel rod which, if held correctly, is supposed to twitch when over hidden water.

Extra-sensory perception, sometimes abbreviated to ESP, refers to those senses beyond our ordinary ones such as sight or smell, with which some people claim to be gifted, for example telepathy.

A *hallucination* is an unreal vision, sometimes caused by the misuse of drugs.

Mummification is the preservation of a corpse, usually by tightly wrapping the body in bandages soaked in special substances.

Phenomena are remarkable or unusual people, things or events. The singular of this noun is *phenomenon*.

A *prediction* is a foretelling of some happening in the future.

Psychic describes something to do with the mind, spirit or soul, and a person who claims to be able to get in touch with the spirit of a dead person is called a psychic.

A *psychoanalyst* investigates illnesses of the mind which are often caused by events that have been forgotten by the patient. The psychoanalyst tries to cure the illness by raising these events from the patient's subconscious and talking about them.

Subconscious refers to the part of our mind that works without our being able to control it. We're not even aware of it working, frequently.

A *superstition* is an unreasonable belief in something. For instance, people still say 'Touch wood', although we no longer believe in the spirits that were reputed to live in trees.

Telepathy is communication between two people's minds without any actual physical form of communication, such as talking or a written message, taking place.

The Many Faces of Fortune-Telling

Man longs to know the future. He searches for it in the stars, in his hands, and in the daily events that surround his life. All unexpected happenings are seen as omens of things to come. To the fortune-teller nothing happens by chance but forms part of a predestined order: a belief that has given birth to many weird and wonderful ways of foretelling the future.

You may have heard of astrology and palmistry. But have you ever heard of moleosophy, axinomancy, or pessomancy?

Moleosophy is a method of divination from the moles on a person's body. A mole on the left side of a woman's face means that she is lucky, but for a man it must be on the right side. A mole on the left knee means that you have a bad temper. If you have one on your right knee it predicts a happy marriage. Even the shape and colour of a mole can give the fortune-teller an indication of your future.

Axinomancy is divination with an axe which can be used for the detection of buried treasure. A precious stone, usually an agate, is placed upon a red-hot axe. If it falls off and rolls in the same direction on three successive occasions, the direction of its fall indicates the whereabouts of the treasure.

Pessomancy is the interpretation of the patterns made by a handful of pebbles dropped on a table. Similar methods use sand, sticks or grain for the same purpose.

Even an ordinary everyday sneeze is an omen to be interpreted. The Ancient Greeks believed a sneeze to be a sign of danger. In Japan it is believed that to sneeze once indicates good luck, to sneeze twice means that you are guilty of some crime and three times is a sign of forthcoming illness.

Michael Scott, Emperor Frederick's astrologer in the 13th century, stated that to sneeze twice in the night on three successive nights was a sign of impending death.

Even the day on which you sneeze is supposed to have a meaning:

Sneeze on a Monday, sneeze for danger;
Sneeze on a Tuesday, kiss a stranger;
Sneeze on a Wednesday, sneeze for a letter;
Sneeze on a Thursday, for something better;
Sneeze on a Friday, sneeze for woe;
Sneeze on a Saturday, a journey to go;
Sneeze on a Sunday, see your lover tomorrow.

Crystal-gazing, or 'scrying', has always been a popular form of fortune-telling. In the majority of cases a crystal ball is used but most shiny objects have proved equally suitable. The Greeks used a mirror, Dr. Dee, a magician of the 16th century,

used a piece of polished coal, the Huille-che tribe of South American indians use a shiny black stone. Some scryers use nothing more than an ordinary glass of water in which they claim to see visions of the future. Even treacle can be used for this purpose!

The Romans put great faith in the art of augury – fortune-telling from the behaviour of birds. Birds flying past the augur from left to right was considered to be a good sign but if they flew in the opposite direction it was bad. Flying towards the augur was good, flying away was bad. The height at which the birds flew had also to be interpreted and, generally speaking, the greater the height the better the omen.

In the year 2737 BC the Chinese Emperor Shen-Nung discovered the art of making tea. Little did he realise that tea-drinking would form the basis of one of the most popular methods of foretelling the future – reading the tea leaves. Before the leaves can be read a traditional ritual must be observed. The inquirer drinks from the cup until only a teaspoonful of liquid remains. With the left hand the cup is turned anti-clockwise three times, inverted on to the saucer and tapped on the base three times with the index finger of the left hand. After a few seconds' wait for the leaves to settle the cup is lifted with the right hand and the patterns formed by the tea leaves left in the cup are interpreted by the fortune-teller.

Almost anything, so it is claimed, can be a portent of the future. But despite all the many

methods of predicting what will happen tomorrow, one question still remains: Do they work?
There is only one way to find out – wait until
tomorrow and see!

Footprints of the Devil

On the morning of February 8th, 1855, the people in Topsham, Lympstone, Exmouth, Teignmouth, Dawlish, and many other Devon villages and towns awoke to a strange and awesome sight. It had snowed heavily during the night, covering the countryside with a thick, glistening white carpet. Nothing marred the peaceful scene except a long line of curious hoofprints in the snow. But these were no ordinary hoofprints.

They could not have been made by a horse, a donkey, or any other four-legged animal, for they consisted of a single track only. The only conclusion that the frightened Devon folk could come to was that they had been made by some one-legged animal. One person suggested that the prints had been made by a kangaroo – but there were no one-legged kangaroos in Devon!

People came from far and wide to see the mystery. Investigations showed that the prints appeared in one continuous line across the countryside for a distance of about 160 kilometres (100 miles). They measured from four to six centimetres across and were evenly spaced about twenty centimetres apart, whether on flat ground

or passing over houses or hayricks. It seemed that nothing had impeded the 'animal's' regular progress.

Not even the three kilometre-wide River Exe had stopped the tracks. They simply ended on one bank and began again on the other side of the water.

Learned men examined the tracks and several wrote to the London newspapers, describing the mystery and giving possible reasons for its cause. Some of the theories were more incredible than the mystery itself.

One man wrote: 'Birds could not have left these marks, as no bird's foot leaves the impression of a hoof, nor, even were there a bird capable of doing so, could it proceed in the direct manner above stated, nor would birds, even if they had donkey's feet, confine themselves to one direct line, but hop here and there; but the nature of the mark at once sets aside its being the track of a bird.

'The effect of the atmosphere upon these marks is given by many as a solution, but how could it be possible for the atmosphere to affect one impression and not another?

'On the morning that the above were observed, the snow bore the fresh marks of cats, dogs, rabbits, birds and men clearly defined. Why, then, should a continuous track, far more clearly defined – so clearly, even, that the raising in the centre of the frog of each foot could be plainly seen – why, then, should this particular mark be the only one which was affected by the atmosphere, and all the others left as they were?'

Other explanations for the mysterious marks included otters, badgers, rats, hares, rabbits, and even frogs.

Another idea was that they were caused by some unknown creature akin to the Loch Ness Monster. But in the minds of the superstitious country folk there was only one answer that was feasible. The tracks must have been made by the Lord of the Underworld – the Devil – and they were very soon known as 'the Devil's hoofmarks'.

One report stated that the footprints were so clear they looked as if they had been burned in the snow. This remark only served to reinforce the idea that these were indeed the footprints of Satan.

Richard Owen, a famous naturalist of the time, put forward the theory that badgers had made the prints. He pointed out that a badger's footprint is formed larger than the badger's foot and that these animals place their hind paws in the same position previously occupied by the front paws. He admitted that no one badger could have made all the prints but that they were probably the result of several badgers searching for food. What he could not explain were the prints that went over haystacks and houses.

According to most versions of the mystery, nothing like it has ever occurred before or since. Further investigation, however, reveals that there have been similar occurrences in different parts of the world.

In the heated correspondence that followed the publication of the Devon story, a man wrote to *The Times* stating that similar tracks were quite common in sand and snow on a particular hill in Poland.

In New Jersey the so-called Jersey Devil has been leaving the same type of track for over a hundred years.

Some reports go even further back in time. On 29th July, 1205, mysterious hoof-like prints were found at Coggeshall following a fierce electrical storm.

The Antarctic explorer, Sir James Ross, discovered what seem to have been prints of the same type near the Antarctic Circle in 1840. Ross sent a party of men ashore to investigate the prints, which he later described as being 'three inches in length and two and a half in breadth, having a small and deeper impression on each side, and the shape of a horseshoe.' Could these prints have been made by the same strange creature that visited Devon fifteen years later?

In 1855, Tom Fox, a Devon man, suggested the prints were made by a rat that jumped from place to place with all its four legs held together. Hence the single line of prints.

In 1968, the naturalist Alfred Leutscher added to the rat theory when he stated: 'An animal, when hopping, lands with all four feet in a bunch, and in soft snow, especially when it is melting, the result is a U-shaped impression – the Devil's footprint.' He then pointed out there is only one British animal small enough to have made the tracks found in Devon, the wood mouse. This creature can climb extremely well and jump high. Leutscher had found wood mouse prints in snow in Epping Forest. These prints match the drawings of the Devon prints so it seems that there is a simple explanation after all – or is there?

In 1924, the explorer James Alan Rennie was in Canada with a French Canadian trapper when they came across strange tracks running across a frozen lake. The tracks, like those in Devon, were equally spaced in a single line and looked as if they had been made by some sort of two-toed bear. The trapper gasped in horror at the sight of the tracks. Rennie asked him what was wrong and the now almost hysterical man explained they were the tracks of Windygo, the Canadian cousin of the Sasquatch.

Later Rennie returned to the lake and actually witnessed the tracks being made – but there was nothing in sight at the time! He was about half a mile from the shore when he saw the tracks appearing in front of him. He could clearly see the imprints of the thing as it came towards him but there was no creature of any sort in sight. Whatever was making the tracks was completely invisible. Rennie stood in frightened amazement as the tracks came closer and closer.

'I stood stock still, filled with reasonless panic,' he said later. 'The tracks were being made within fifty yards of me – twenty – ten – then, smack! I shouted aloud as a large blob of water hit me in the face. I swung round brushing the water from my eyes and saw the tracks continuing across the lake.'

Had the mysterious tracks been made by an animal – or *something else?* We can try and explain them away, but we still don't know for certain . . .

What a Coincidence!

Coincidence is such a part of everyday life that we do not take much notice of it. If you are thinking of a friend as the telephone rings and it is the same friend on the other end of the line you may comment on it, but most people do not attach much importance to such occurrences. But some co-incidences are so strange that it seems there is some unseen force causing them to happen.

The author J. B. Priestley once described a strange experience his wife Jacquetta Hawkes, the archaeologist, had had.

'My wife bought three large coloured drawings by Graham Sutherland. When they arrived from London she took them up to her bedroom to hang them up in the morning. They were leaning against a chair and the one on the outside, facing the room, was a drawing of a grasshopper. When Jacquetta got into bed that night, she felt some sort of twittering movement going on, so she got out and pulled back the clothes. There was a grasshopper in the bed. No grasshopper had been seen in that room before, nor has been seen since. No grasshopper has ever been seen at any other time in the house.'

In 1953, Irving Kupcinet, an American journalist, visited London following a visit to Paris, to report on the coronation of Elizabeth II. Much to his surprise he found in a drawer in his hotel bedroom some personal belongings of his friend Harry Hannin, a player in the Harlem Globe-trotters' basketball team. Two days later something even more surprising happened – he received a letter from Hannin, who was in Paris. The letter said: 'You'll never believe this, Irving, but I have just found a tie with your name on it in my hotel bedroom!'

Early this century in London, three men were hanged for the murder of Sir Edmundbury Godfrey. The murder took place at Greenberry Hill and the surnames of the three men were Green, Berry, and Hill.

When he was at school in Orleans, the French poet Emile Deschamps met a Monsieur de Fortgibu who had just returned from England. While in England de Fortgibu had acquired a taste for plum pudding and begged Deschamps to try it. The poet enjoyed the dish but forgot all about it until ten years later when he passed a restaurant in which he could see a plum pudding being prepared. Remembering how much he had enjoyed it on the first occasion, Deschamps went into the restaurant to buy it. 'I am sorry, Monsieur,' said the restauranteur, 'But this dish is being especially made for someone.' Deschamps decided to wait for the customer to see if he would be prepared to sell the pudding, or at least a slice of it. When the customer arrived, who should it be but de Fortgibu!

Many years later, Deschamps was invited to a dinner party. One of the delicacies on the menu was English plum pudding. Naturally the poet told his fellow diners about the previous two occasions on which he had had the dish. 'Wouldn't it be strange,' said his friends, 'if de Fortgibu turned up now!' and they all laughed. But the laughter turned to astonishment later in the evening. Monsieur de Fortgibu came into the room! He had been invited to the meal but had lost his way. 'My goodness!' exclaimed Emile Deschamps, 'Only three times have I eaten plum pudding and each time I have met Monsieur de Fortgibu.'

A remarkable series of coincidences mark the life of King Umberto I of Italy. In July, 1900, he visited Monza and was dining at a restaurant when it was pointed out that the owner was the King's double. Interested by this coincidence, the King called the man over and much to his amazement discovered that his name also was Umberto. The coincidence did not end there, however, for it turned out that both men had been born in Turin on the same day. The names of both wives was Margherita, and each had a son named Vittorio. On the very same day that Umberto had been crowned his double had opened the restaurant in Monza.

The following day the King had to attend an athletics meeting and he invited his double to come along. But when he arrived at the stadium the King was informed that the restaurateur had been shot that morning in a mysterious gun accident. Later that same day King Umberto himself was dead, shot by an assassin.

An amazing string of coincidences link the two American presidents, Abraham Lincoln and John F. Kennedy, both of whom were assassinated. Lincoln's assassin, John Wilkes Booth, was born in 1839; Kennedy's assassin, Lee Harvey Oswald, was born in 1939. Abraham Lincoln was elected to office in 1860; Kennedy in 1960.

Both presidents were succeeded by a man named Johnson. Andrew Johnson, who succeeded Lincoln, was born in 1806; Lyndon Johnson was born in 1906.

Both presidents were shot in the head from behind, both on a Friday, and both in the presence of their wives.

Lincoln's secretary, whose name was Kennedy, advised him not to go to the theatre; Kennedy's secretary, whose name was Lincoln, advised him not to go to Dallas.

And as if there were not coincidences enough already, the names Lincoln and Kennedy each contain seven letters; the names Andrew Johnson and Lyndon Johnson each contain thirteen letters; and John Wilkes Booth and Lee Harvey Oswald each contain fifteen letters!

In 1912, the trans-Atlantic liner, the *Titanic*, was hit by an iceberg on her maiden voyage and sank. In 1898, Morgan Robertson wrote a novel, *Futility*, in which a liner, also on its maiden voyage, is sunk by an iceberg in the same area that the *Titanic* was to sink fourteen years later. The name of the vessel in the story was the *Titan*. In 1939, a man at the helm of a ship sailing in the same part of the Atlantic had a sudden feeling that he should stop the vessel. He did so, just in time, for a second later an iceberg appeared and struck the ship, damaging it but causing no loss of life. The name of the vessel on this occasion was the *Titanian*. And the lookout had been born on the very day that the *Titanic* sank!

An even more remarkable coincidence connected with the sea occurred in 1882, when the Brazilian gunboat *Araguary* fished a bottle out of the sea. Inside the bottle was the message: 'Aboard the schooner *Sea Hero*. The crew has mutinied – killing the captain and flinging the first mate overboard. I am the second mate and have been spared to navigate the ship. They are forcing me to head for the Amazon River, 28 long. 22 lat. making 2½ knots. Rush help.'

The message was undated, but as the *Araguay* was not far away from the position indicated, the captain decided to give chase. After two hours' sailing, the *Sea Hero* was sighted near the position given. The captain of the gunboat ordered the other vessel to heave to, and to make sure the order would be obeyed, he fired a shot across the bows. A boarding party went aboard the *Sea Hero*, arrested the mutineers and rescued the second mate.

Although naturally pleased at being rescued, the second mate was somewhat curious as to how the gunboat captain had known of his plight. 'We picked up the note you sent,' explained the captain. 'But I did not send any note!' replied the mystified seaman, 'I've been locked in my cabin

ever since the outbreak of the mutiny.'

When he was shown the note, he expressed even more mystification. It was not until the subsequent court trial that the mystery was explained. The *Sea Hero* had been named after a novel by John Parminton published some sixteen years previously. To publicise the novel the author had dispatched five thousand bottles, each containing a message, into the sea. It was one of these that the crew of the *Araguary* had picked up. A lucky coincidence for the second mate of the *Sea Hero*, but one that defies rational explanation.

Possibly the most amazing case of coincidence occurred during the Second World War. On 2nd May, 1944, one of the clues in the *Daily Telegraph* crossword was : 'One of the U.S.' The answer, revealed in the newspaper the following day, was *Utah*. A short while later the answer to one of the clues was the name of another American state, *Omaha*. This attracted the attention of MI5 for, besides being American states, *Utah* and *Omaha* were the code names given to two beaches to be used in the planned invasion of France, the landings that were later to be known as D-Day.

At this stage MI5 decided to do nothing as the answers could have come about due to pure coincidence. But a few days later they became convinced that the crossword was being used to transmit secret messages to enemy agents when the clue 'This bush is the centre of nursery revolutions' appeared. The answer was *Mulberry*, and this was the codeword for a special pre-fabricated floating harbour that was to be used by the invasion forces. And a couple of days after that one of the crossword answers was *Neptune*, the codeword for the naval operations during the D-Day landings.

Agents were rushed down to Leatherhead in Surrey to interview Leonard Dawe, the schoolmaster who had compiled the crosswords. But after intensive cross examination, it turned out that he was not a German spy and that the names had occurred purely by chance. What a coincidence!

Are There Fairies at the Bottom of Your Garden?

'When the first baby laughed for the first time, his laugh broke into a million pieces, and they all went skipping about. That was the beginning of fairies.'

That was how J. M. Barrie, in his *Little White Bird*, romantically described the creation of fairies. Other authorities have suggested that 'the little people' are the spirits of those who lived before the birth of Christ. Because of the sins they committed as mortals, they were barred from Heaven but were not considered bad enough to enter Hell. Robert Kirk, in his *Secret Commonwealth*, published in 1691, states that they are 'of a middle Nature betwixt Man and Angel.'

Another theory claims that they were originally druids 'transformed because they would not abandon their idolatrous rites, and on that account they are continually growing smaller until they will eventually turn into ants.'

Disbelievers scornfully state that fairies are nothing but 'man's attempt to explain or rationalise natural phenomena.' Primitive man, in his efforts to understand the forces of nature, imagined that spirits inhabited the trees, flowers, waters, and winds of his world. These spirits are embodied in the creatures we now call fairies.

The word 'fairy' is derived from the Old French faer – 'to enchant' – which is, in turn, derived from the Latin fata – 'the fates.' The 'little folk' are well-known all over the world. The hada live in Spain, the fée in France, the fee in Germany and the fata in Italy. In Japan lives the flower fairy Ko-no-hana-sakuya-himo, 'the lady who causes the trees to bloom'. The chief fairy of China is the Ma-Ku, who in the 2nd century reclaimed some land from the sea and transformed it into an orchard of mulberry bushes. The good fairy of Scandinavia is the beautiful vila who maps the future of babies and warns people of approaching death.

The most famous figure in Ireland's fairy folk-lore is the leprechaun, the fairy cobbler. William Allingham described him thus:

> 'He's a span and a quarter in height,
> A wizen'd, bearded elf,
> Spectacles stuck on his pointed nose,
> Silver buckles on his hose,
> Leather apron – shoe in lap.'

Mortals seldom outwit the leprechaun. If by chance you should happen to catch one, hold him tight for he will try all manner of tricks to get away. But hold him with an uninterrupted gaze and eventually he will give in and reveal the whereabouts of his crock of gold.

The fairies of folklore and the fairies of children's stories are inextricably intertwined. The ancient fairies were both good and bad, sometimes friendly to humans but also cruel and dangerous. It was considered to be unlucky to speak of them, so they were called by names such as 'the good folk,' 'the people of peace,' 'the gentle people,' and similar euphemisms.

These original fairies, it was believed, had their own realm beneath the surface of the earth. Oberon and Titania were king and queen of this nether world, and they lived in an enchanted palace with walls made from spiders' legs, windows of cats' eyes and a roof of bats' wings painted with moonbeams.

In 1550, Giovanni Straparola, an Italian, published a collection of traditional fairy folktales. It included the now familiar story of *Puss in Boots*. About 150 years later in France, Charles Perrault published his *Tales of Mother Goose*, which included such favourites as *Cinderella*, *Red Riding Hood* and *The Sleeping Beauty*. In the 1800s Jacob and Wilhelm Grimm published in Germany their *Grimm's Fairy Tales*. And 1872 saw the publication in Denmark of Hans Christian Andersen's famous fairy stories. Twentieth century authors continue to stir the mixture of tradition and make-believe.

Have you ever seen a fairy? Many people claim to have done so. John Kerr of Paisley in Scotland saw some in Largs. One hot afternoon during the summer of 1934, he was walking through the grounds of the Hills Hotel with another resident. A short distance away from them they saw wispy shapes dancing around the flowers. Closer in-

vestigation revealed the forms to be a group of fairies gambolling in the sunlight. It was later confirmed by the hotel manager that other guests had seen them on previous occasions.

In the Irish village of Ballisodare a woman lived with 'the people of the hills' for seven years. The whole of that time she spent in dancing and merrymaking. When she returned home she had no toes – continual dancing had worn them away!

In the 1920s fairies were actually photographed by sisters Elsie and Frances Griffiths. Their pictures have been the cause of constant argument ever since. Conan Doyle, an enthusiastic spiritualist, firmly believed the photographs to be genuine. In his book, *The Coming Of The Fairies*, published in 1922, he said 'they represent either the most elaborate and ingenious hoax ever played upon the public, or else they constitute an event in human history which may in future appear to have been epoch-making in its character.' Interviewed on television in February, 1971, Elsie Griffiths said of the fairies in the pictures: 'If you think very seriously about a thing it will actually become solid. I believe they were figments of our imagination.'

In the British Isles the pixies live in Cornwall, the siths in Scotland, and the sidhe in Ireland. The tylwyth teg of Wales live at the foot of a mountain in Brecon. Any person who can find, and has the courage to go through, the secret doorway to fairyland is royally entertained. The fairies will enchant their visitor with captivating music and joyous dancing. He or she will be decorated with flowers, feasted on fruit and invited to stay for as long as he wishes.

There even could be fairies at the bottom of your garden. So get out your camera (no doubt a Brownie is best) and start clicking around the compost. You never know what may develop!

Charming

There used to be two classes of charms – amulets, which protected the wearer from the evil eye, and talismans, which were primarily luck-bringers. Nowadays the two meanings have fused and are interchangeable. A modern charm bracelet holds a sufficient and varied number of amulets and talismans to ward off all but the most determined of evil spirits and should attract every bit of good luck that is going.

Animals have played an important role in the history of amulets and talismans. Most popular of animal amulets is the cat, regarded as a powerful force since the days of ancient Egypt, when the creature was considered sacred to the goddess Bast. Charms in the shape of a lizard are reputed to give the wearer infinite wisdom and excellent eyesight. A frog amulet ensures a happy relationship between lovers. To the Romans the frog was the symbol of Aphrodite, the goddess of love, and brought health, wealth, and fertility to the owner. In Greece frog charms are worn to ward off ill-health. In Burma they are worn by children to protect them from evil.

The magical powers of the horse are embodied

in the horsebrass and horseshoe. Horsebrasses were used originally to prevent witches from halting horses in their tracks, as witches were wont to do. The modern equivalent of the horsebrass is the mass of badges decorating the motor car. Badges of all shapes and sizes now take the place of the horsebrasses of yesteryear, and in the driver's subconscious fulfil the same function.

Horseshoes are thought to be lucky because they are the same shape as the crescent moon. This shape has always been associated with mother-hood and good fortune. Another explanation relates an encounter between Saint Dunstan and the Devil. One day the Devil asked Saint Dunstan to shoe one of his hooves, for the Saint was an expert blacksmith. Although the Saint agreed to do this, he caused the Devil so much pain that he cried out to be released. 'I will release you,' said the Saint, 'Provided that you promise to avoid all places where a horseshoe is hung.' The Devil, who was now in considerable agony, readily agreed to the suggestion. Ever since that time, horseshoes have acted as a protection against the forces of evil. It is up to you whether or not you believe that story, but there is one point of which you must be careful. If you hang up a horseshoe, always position it with the points uppermost. According to tradition, if you hang it upside down all the luck will run out.

Before the Battle of Trafalgar, Nelson, it is said, nailed a horseshoe to the mast of HMS *Victory*. Modern yachtsmen still do the same, as do fisher-men in many parts of the British Isles. Horseshoe replicas can be found in abundance at weddings, given in the hope that they will bring luck and happiness to the blushing bride. A number of American salesmen carry a miniature horseshoe in their case of samples. Whether or not this results in increased sales is not recorded.

All metal objects exert some form of influence in the world of magic. This is mainly due to the fact that the first metals were discovered in meteorites. It was naturally assumed that as these had fallen from the sky they must have been sent by the gods and would therefore possess magical properties.

Each metal was associated with a particular planet and considered to be most powerful when engraved with the appropriate astrological symbol. The sign for Saturn drawn on lead brought well-being in childbirth. Gold, the metal of the sun, engraved with the astrological symbol of the sun, ensured good fortune, admiration and friends in high places. Luna tables were most effective when inscribed on silver.

Being made of metal, coins are also considered to possess magical properties. Probably the most famous of talismanic coins is the Lee Penny, a silver groat with a red triangular stone set in its centre. Reputed to have originated in 14th century Spain, it is said to have the power of healing. Sir Simon Locard of Lee obtained the talisman whilst in Spain and it has remained in the hands of the Scottish family of Lockharts ever since. In the 1930's a guest of Sir Simon Lockhart cut his hand very badly. Nothing could stop the bleeding, so it was decided to test the powers of the Lee Penny. Sir Simon dipped the coin three times in a basin of water, the time-honoured method of harnessing the coin's power. The guest placed his bloody hand in the charged water and the bleeding ceased. Within a very short time the cut had healed completely.

Royalty has always been a great believer in the supernatural. Catherine of Aragon was forewarned of Henry VIII's waning affection when the stone in her ruby ring turned a deeper shade of red. Ferdinand I of Spain carried a piece of coral which he pointed at persons he suspected of secret evil intentions. Charles I owned a charm bearing a magical inscription written for him by Pope Leo IX. The inscription read: 'Who that beareth it upon him shall not dread his enemies to be overcome, nor with no manner of poison be hurt, nor in no need misfortune, nor with no thunder he shall not be smitten nor lightning, nor in no fire be burnt soddainly, nor in no water be drowned. Nor he shall not die without shrift, nor with theeves to be taken. Also he shall have no wrong neither of Lord or Lady. This be in the names of God and Christ * Messias * Sother * Emannell * Sabaoth.'

King John of England owned four magical rings, a gift from Pope Innocent. The letter accompanying the gift explained its importance: 'Their roundness denotes eternity, the number four, which is a square, signifies firmness of mind, not to be shaken by adversity nor elevated by prosperity. . . . By the gold is signified wisdom, as gold is the most precious of metals, wisdom is of all endowments the most precious. . . . The green colour of the emerald denotes faith; the clearness of the sapphire hope; the redness of the ruby charity; and the colour of the opal good works. In the emerald, therefore, you have what you are to believe; in the sapphire what you are to hope; in the ruby what you are to love; and in the opal what you are to practise.'

A large number of charms have consisted of magic words written on parchment. The most famous of these was the word 'Abracadabra' which was used to ward off illness. Daniel Defoe in his *Journal of the Plague Year* mentions the fact that many Londoners used this charm as a protection from the plague of 1665. The parchment was carried in a small bag which was worn on a thong around the neck.

To be most effective, the magic word Abracadabra has to be written as an inverted triangle like this:

ABRACADABRA
ABRACADABR
ABRACADAB
ABRACADA
ABRACAD
ABRACA
ABRAC
ABRA
ABR
AB
A

The word was written down in this fashion because it was believed that as the word gradually disappeared into nothing so, too, would the illness fade away.

Belief in such things still exists. Even in this so-called 'civilised' age we are bound by ancient superstitions. People still throw spilt salt over their left shoulder to blind the Devil, avoid walking beneath ladders and believe they will have seven years' bad luck when they smash a mirror. You, of course, do not believe in all this supernatural 'stuff and nonsense', but it is a fair bet that several of your friends carry in their handbags or pockets some form of good luck token. A large proportion of the population pin their faith on such luck-bringers as a rabbit's foot, Saint Christopher medallion or lucky mascot.

Possibly the most popular luck-bringer in the Western world is the four-leafed clover. This is said to be lucky because each of the four leaves has an influence over one of the four forces that control fame, wealth, health, and love. A more likely reason for the four-leafed clover's association with good luck is that in normal conditions it is rather rare. If you do find a four-leaf clover it is essential to pick it at midnight on a Friday during the first three days of a new moon. If this is not possible, it is said to be just as effective if picked in a grave-yard between noon and three p.m. on a sunny day!

You would think that educated people would have no need for superstition, and yet every university has its mascot. You have only to watch ITV's 'University Challenge' for a few weeks for proof of this. In the shots of the audience at the end of the show you can always see a mascot in pride of place!

We have a basic need for reassurance when faced with the unknown. Just as the baby grasps its teddy bear when frightened, so do adults turn to religion and the supernatural in moments of insecurity. And even some of the most disbelieving of people have at some time in their lives relied upon some lucky object. They often work merely because the owner believes in their power. But who knows? There *may* be supernatural forces at work in these things and it can do no harm to carry an amulet or talisman. It may even bring you a bit of good luck!

Strange Men of the Mountains

In 1951, Eric Shipton and Michael Ward were walking along the edge of the Menlung Glacier in the Himalayas, returning from an Everest Reconnaissance Mission, when they came across some unusual footprints in the snow. Shipton took a photograph of one of the prints and even had the presence of mind to place his ice pick alongside it to show its size.

The type of footprint that Shipton photographed was already well-known to mountaineers. There had also been several reports of strange creatures seen in the mountains. And to the people who lived in the region, such creatures had been regarded as fact for many hundreds of years.

In the Western world the creature is often called 'the Abominable Snowman'. This is a translation of 'Metch Kangmi' which is what the Tibetans call the creature. Another name for the creature is the 'Yeti'. This is the name given to it by the sherpas, who believe it to be a descendant of an ancient monkey king who once lived in the mountains. The king fell in love with an ogress and their children were the ancestors of the present day yeti.

Descriptions of the creature vary and it may be that, if it does exist, there are several varieties. Generally speaking, however, the creature is said to be about 155 centimetres high. It walks erect like a human but its arms reach right down to its knees. The whole of its body is covered with light brown, or reddish, hair and it is said to have rather a pungent and revolting smell. The only noise that the yeti is said to make is a series of roars, whistles, and yelps.

The yeti appears in many of the folk tales of the hardy people who live in the Himalayas. In one such story a yeti was captured by the villagers of the Jalap-La Valley in Sikkim. The villagers put out a bucket containing an alcoholic beverage and this apparently lured the creature out into the open. After drinking the liquid the creature became intoxicated and eventually passed out. As soon as this happened the villagers rushed forward and bound the creature with strong ropes. They then carried it in triumphant procession into the village. Unfortunately, and presumably inevitably, when they came to look at it the following day they found only the ropes – the creature had escaped back to the mountains.

Major L. A. Waddell appears to have been the first European to witness the tracks of the yeti. These he saw in Sikkim in 1889, but as there is no description of the tracks it is difficult to establish exactly what he saw. His sherpas told him that the tracks he discovered were those of the yeti, but it is possible that they said this only to please the Major, who was rather sceptical regarding the existence of such strange creatures.

Thirty years before Shipton took his famous photograph, Lieutenant-Colonel C. K. Howard-Bury, leader of the First Everest Reconnaissance Expedition in 1921, had reported seeing similar prints. They were sighted on the Lhakpa-La at a height of around 6,100 metres.

Howard-Bury described the incident as follows: 'Even at these heights we came across tracks in the snow. We were able to pick out tracks of hares and foxes, but one that at first looked like a human foot puzzled us considerably. Our coolies at once jumped to the conclusion that this must be "The Wild Man of the Snows", to which they gave the name of Metch-kangmi, the Abominable Snowman who interested the newspapers so much on my return to civilised countries. ... These tracks, which caused so much comment, were probably caused by a large "loping" greywolf, which in the soft snow formed double tracks rather like those of a barefooted man.'

Following Howard-Bury's report in the English newspapers, there was a flood of correspondence from people claiming to have seen the creature. At about the same time there were also a large number of letters in newspapers from people who had claimed to have witnessed the legendary Indian Rope Trick. Coincidence? Or could it have been brought about by the fact that people at that time wanted to believe in something out of the ordinary?

In view of the immense publicity the creature received in the 1920s, it seems strange that it did not achieve a world-wide sensation until the publication of Shipton's photograph. Of course, it was not until the twentieth century that the news media was advanced enough to cope with such stories. But even so you cannot help receiving the impression that the yeti, and indeed the Loch Ness Monster, are modern inventions and that local stories, which abound in all parts of the globe, have been used to add 'meat' to what is a purely fictional story. It is quite possible that the reports of witnesses were given in good faith. But if you are told that you are likely to see a monster in a particular place, you will think any shadowy or slightly mysterious object you see *is* the monster.

Seven years after the first successful ascent of Everest, the leader of that expedition, Sir Edmund Hillary, led another expedition in the Himalayas. Its primary purpose was to discover the effects that living in such inhospitable conditions for a length of time would have on the human body. But Hillary was also determined to be the first man to capture a yeti, and he and his party spent a great deal of time searching for the mysterious creature. Part of the yeti hunting equipment consisted of guns that fired darts. These had been tipped with curare, a paralysing poison from South America.

They found a great number of tracks but never caught sight of the creature that made them. They did, however, bring back two yeti scalps belonging to a Nepalese monastery. When examined by experts, however, it was found that the scalps, although of great age, had been made from goat skins!

47

Another mountaineer, Don Williams, actually saw the yeti in 1970. He was in the Himalayas at a height of 4,000 metres, photographing some strange animal tracks. At the end of the day he actually saw a creature that could have made the tracks. It looked like an ape, moved on all fours, and was clearly seen in the light of the full moon.

In 1975, Lhakpa Sherpani, a teenage Nepalese shepherd girl, reported that her cow and four of her yaks had been attacked by a yeti. She got a good look at the creature as it attacked her animals. 'It had a black face,' she said. 'And it looked something like a man, but it had black and brown hair with a white strip running down its chest to the stomach. Another white strip ran from the centre of its forehead to the top of its head. Its eyebrows were grey and thick and it had round eyes, like those of an ox. Its lips were black and the mouth was large with big white teeth, like human teeth. The fingers were thick with long nails and its feet looked like human feet, except they were covered with hair.'

What had the girl seen? The local police were convinced that it was the legendary yeti. They examined footprints and handprints found at the scene and the animals that had been slaughtered. They came to the conclusion that whatever had attacked Lhakpa's animals was large, powerful, and heavy – it certainly was not human.

Similar creatures seem to live all over the world. In Africa there is a strange creature called the Chemosit; in China, the Hsileh-Jen; and there is the Almas that apparently lives in Russia.

It has been reported that, in 1941, a party of Russian soldiers searching for deserters captured an almas. The soldiers were not sure what to make of the growling fur-covered beast, so they called in a doctor to make an examination. The Doctor, Lieutenant-Colonel Vazgen Karapetyan, described the body of the 'man' as being 'covered with dark brown fur, with light brown hair on his face, like a calf. He was about five feet ten inches tall, wide-chested and broad-shouldered. When I pulled hair from his body he growled.'

Karapetyan told the soldiers they had caught not a deserter but some form of primitive creature. But after the doctor had left, the poor unfortunate creature was executed as a deserter by a firing squad. The report ends with the fact that no-one now knows what happened to the creature's body. This is a frequent ending to such stories all over the world. So once again we are left with no positive proof as to the creature's existence.

Early in 1978, the Soviet News Agency, Tass, reported that villagers in the Verkhoyansk region of Russia were being scared by a manlike monster. The descriptions of this creature were more or less the same as for the yeti and the almas. Villagers were warned not to go out at night in case the creature should attack them.

The American cousin of the yeti and the almas is the sasquatch, or 'bigfoot' as he is more commonly known. Several organised searches have been made for the sasquatch, but the mountainous country in which it is said to live is difficult to explore. As a result the searches have never lasted for very long and have so far proved nothing. Caves have been found that showed signs of recent habitation but it is possible that these were the homes of hermits – who can say?

There is a story that a sasquatch was captured and displayed in the late 1800's. The creature, nicknamed Jacko, was found lying next to a railway track in 1884. According to contemporary reports it was half man and half animal. With the exception of its hands and feet it was covered from top to bottom in long dark hair. It was put on exhibition in Yale but, as with all good monster stories, no trace of the creature exists today and no-one seems to know exactly what happened to it, although many people claim to have seen it.

The best known encounter with a sasquatch was that of Albert Ostmann, a gold prospector, in 1924. One night he suddenly woke up with the feeling that he was being bundled around in his sleeping bag. Then he realised that he was being carried through the night by some huge creature. Naturally, he struggled, but his captor, who was some two and a half metres high, was far too strong for him.

After travelling what he thought was about 25 miles Ostmann was slung to the ground. Slowly he rose to his feet to find that the creature had been joined by what were apparently its wife and family. The smallest of the beasts was at least two metres high and all were covered with hair. The creatures did not appear to wish the prospector any harm for they seemed to be more curious than aggressive. They were particularly intrigued with the man's equipment, for it seemed they had no concept of tools of any sort.

For six days Ostmann was held captive. Eventually he managed to escape by a piece of sheer good luck. One of the creatures tried to eat his snuffbox and became ill. In the following confusion the prospector made his escape and eventual return to civilisation.

The sasquatch has been photographed many times but possibly the most convincing record of the creature is a film made by Robert Patterson. Shot on 20 October, 1967, the film shows an ape-like creature walking upright about 30 metres away from the camera. The film has been examined by experts but no evidence of trickery has been discovered.

One of the best pieces of evidence in support of the existence of the sasquatch was found in 1969 near Bossburgh, Washington. It consisted of a series of footprints, 1,089 of them in all, that could be followed for a distance of half a mile. Each print was 18 centimetres wide and 43 centimetres long and it was evident from the prints that the right foot had been injured.

If creatures such as the yeti, almas, and sasquatch exist and are of such considerable size, why is it that not one of the many expeditions raised to find them has succeeded in capturing one? Not only that, but they have never succeeded in finding any physical evidence of the creatures' existence. One explanation could be that the creatures are scared of man and so avoid any contact. Another reason is that the areas in which these creatures are said to exist are mountainous and inhospitable, making all such expeditions expensive and dangerous.

The theory that these creatures are monkeys or bears appears to be supported by many descriptions of the beasts. As an example, consider this description made by N. A. Tombazi who saw a yeti near the Zemu Glacier. It was 'about two to three hundred yards away down the valley to the east of our camp. Unquestionably the figure in outline was exactly like a human being, walking upright and stopping occasionally to uproot or pull at some dwarf rhododendron bushes. It showed up dark against the snow and, as far as I could make out, wore no clothes. Within the next minute or so it had moved into some thick scrub and was lost to view.' Later Tombazi returned to the spot to examine the footprints left by the creature he had seen. From the descriptions he gave, most experts now believe that what he saw was not a yeti but a bear.

One day we may establish whether or not such creatures really do exist. As Ralph Izzard of the 1954 yeti expedition once wrote: 'It is hard indeed to escape from the view that there is in these remote, vast and unexplored ranges, some beast as yet unknown to science.' Could there really be some hitherto unknown creature roaming the remote corners of the world or have we created these strange beasts in our imagination? Perhaps we will never know for certain – until one of them is captured.

In the meantime should you yourself ever

encounter a yeti, and presumably the same will hold true of the sasquatch and similar creatures, follow the advice given by Tibetan parents to their children! 'If you see a yeti always run down-hill. This will make the creature's long hair fall over its eyes so it will be unable to see you and you can then make your escape.'

All In the Mind

'That ship is going to sink,' cried Mrs. Marshall, as the magnificent trans-Atlantic liner steamed out of the harbour. Friends rushed forward to comfort her. 'Don't worry,' they said, 'That ship has been built to the very latest design. It is absolutely unsinkable.'

But they were unable to calm down Mrs. Marshall. She only became even more hysterical. 'Oh, can't you stop them,' she groaned. 'All the people will be drowned.'

Five days later, on 14th April, 1912, Mrs. Marshall's prophecy came true. The ship, the *Titanic*, struck an iceberg and over fifteen hundred people lost their lives.

Such prediction of future events is quite common but the big question is: 'what causes it?' Is it just one of the coincidences of life or is there something more to it than that? Could it be that humans have the power of telepathy? Many people believe telepathy to be a fact. Unfortunately laboratory experiments to examine such mysteries tend to be disappointing.

Because only certain people achieve good scores in such tests many believe that extra-

sensory perception is a gift bestowed only on certain individuals. This is probably not the case. It is more than likely that each and every one of us possesses telepathic powers to a certain extent but that some, through either upbringing, environment or experience, have developed these powers to a higher degree than normal.

Judging from recent research it would seem that telepathy, if it does exist, is a primitive form of communication, one that civilised man has forgotten how to use. It is quite likely that early man used some form of telepathy as a means of communication but when he began to use language this extra sensory perception was no longer necessary. As a result modern man has forgotten how to use this particular function of his brain. This is borne out by the fact that experiments with very young children usually give quite promising results but as they grow older they tend to lose the ability.

One of the factors that seems to affect results in experiments is whether or not the subject himself believes that telepathy is a possibility. If a person is sceptical then the score achieved will be considerably lower than that of someone who believes that such powers are possible.

The term 'extra sensory perception' is a general expression that covers four types of phenomena – telepathy, precognition, clairvoyance, and psychokinesis. Telepathy is mind to mind contact between two or more persons; precognition is the ability to foresee the future, clairvoyance is the ability to see through or beyond an object, and psychokinesis is the ability to move or influence an inanimate object by the power of the mind. Most researchers believe that all four aspects are results of the same psychic ability.

But there is always one question that remains unanswered. Is extra-sensory perception a possibility? Well, there is a mass of evidence that points to the fact that it is a reality. Unfortunately, not many people have yet discovered how to develop this ability to the full so that experimental results can be verified at will. American and Russian scientists, however, are convinced that this can be achieved and are carrying out experiments to discover if such communication can be used for military purposes.

Here is a technique you can try to see whether or not your sixth sense is well developed. Simply take a pack of playing cards and give it a good shuffle. Now lay out the first twenty cards, face down, in two rows of ten cards each.

Look at the first card, touch it if you like, and then write down any impression you receive of the card. You may feel you know what colour it is, or just a number will come into your mind. At other times you will have a feeling it is a picture card. Sometimes the name of a suit will come to mind. If you feel really lucky you may think of both a suit and a value. Whatever comes to mind write it down. Do not try to concentrate too hard as that will only destroy any latent extra sensory abilities you may have. Write down the first thing that comes into your head. Now try the next card and continue in the same fashion until you have guessed something for each of the twenty cards.

Now comes the revelation! Turn each card face up and compare the cards with your list. If you have more than six correct guesses out of twenty you have done better than could be expected by pure chance. Such a result indicates that you could have psychic tendencies. Over eight correct means that you are very definitely telepathic. If you try this test several times and you consistently score eight or more correct you have telepathic powers worthy of further investigation. If you, or your friends upon whom you try this test, consistently score more than ten it is a sign that someone is cheating!

Things That Go Bump in the Night

In the summer of 1965, Peter and Irene Nierman
moored their barge at a wharf on the River Maas
near Tertogenbosch, in Holland. Peter had gone
ashore leaving Irene and their five-year-old son
Willem on board. Irene was watching Willem
walking across the deck when suddenly his feet
slipped and he plunged into the fast-flowing water.
Irene screamed and ran to the rail of the barge.
There was little she could do, for she was pregnant,
and instinctively she knew there was no hope of
saving her son.

Her screams alerted some workmen on the
wharf and they ran to help. But there was little
chance of their getting to the boy in time. Describing the incident later, Irene Nierman said: 'I was
certain there was nothing anyone could do. No
one could reach him. It was as though it was
decreed that my son would die.

'Then suddenly by the piles alongside the ware-
houses I saw a man. At first it was as though I
sensed him rather than saw him and then I could
see he was a tall, black-haired man, in a dark
overall.

'Although I never took my eyes off him, I never

actually saw him jump into the water, but the next minute he was there, alongside Willem, lifting him out of the water and cradling him in his arms.'

Irene ran from the barge and on to the wharf, where the man had now managed to get the boy ashore. Joyously she hugged her son, who had so miraculously been saved. Tears of joy welled up in her eyes as she turned to thank the man . . . but he was already hurrying away. Then the dock workers ran to her and when she looked again the mysterious stranger had vanished. The dockers asked Irene what she was looking at and she told them of the rescue which they had not actually seen. When she described the man who had saved her son the dockers became suddenly silent. Irene was so overjoyed at having Willem safe and sound she did not notice their silence and the strange looks they were giving one another.

The following day Peter Nierman tried to find the stranger in order to thank him. He, too, met the same wall of silence and the strange looks. Eventually he asked the dockers what was wrong. 'Well,' said one. 'Your description fits Johan Udink.'

'Fine!' replied Peter. 'Where can I find him?'

'You won't find him,' said the docker. 'He died ten years ago yesterday. He was drowned at the very same spot that your son fell into the water . . .'

Did a ghost save the drowning boy's life or was it pure coincidence that the stranger looked like the man that had drowned there ten years previously? Who can tell? It may well be a fact that ghosts exist, for there is certainly a wealth of evidence to support the idea.

Stories of ghosts go right back to the beginnings of recorded history. Without counting, you could estimate that there must be millions upon millions of ghosts reported around the world. Whilst it is accepted that many of these are at the worst lies and at the best good stories, one is left with an impressive number of authenticated accounts that seem to prove that ghosts exist. If one then takes away from these all those genuine stories that could have a natural explanation, there still remains an immensely large number for which there appears to be no rational explanation.

Descriptions of ghosts vary but it is interesting to find that in many cases the observer thought they were seeing a normal live person, until perhaps the image disappeared, whereupon the observer realised that he or she had seen a ghost. Other ghosts are little more than shadowy or wispy shapes that appear to have no definite form.

Most ghosts are of human form but there are many recorded instances of spirit animals having been seen. In a large number of cases the dead person appearing as a ghost is related to the observer. Usually such visions occur soon after the person's death – emotion being almost a vital factor in the creation of a ghost.

It would seem that the majority of ghosts are harmless and in fact very few of them seem aware that they are being observed. On a few occasions ghosts have been said to speak to the observer but this is quite a rare occurrence.

A particularly interesting form of ghost is the poltergeist. This type of ghost throws objects around the room, disturbs furniture, causes strange noises, and so on. It was once thought that a poltergeist was a playful ghost but then it became increasingly obvious that in a large majority of cases the strange activity occurred only in the vicinity of one person – usually a young person.

Emotion seems to be mysteriously connected with ghosts. In the majority of cases where a ghost is said to exist there is a dramatic story attached to that person's life or death. In a large number of cases this emotion is violent or bad but this is not the case with all ghosts. Some ghosts appear to visit a site because it has happy memories for them.

Because of the emotion and bloodshed involved in war, old battle grounds are a constant source of ghost sightings. One such battle ground is that of Marston Moor, between York and Knaresborough, where a battle was fought on 2nd July, 1644, during the English Civil War.

In the late 1930s a commercial traveller, Thomas Horner, and a colleague, Arthur Wright, were driving across the moor when a bus approached from the opposite direction. Horner had moved well over to the left to allow the bus plenty of room to pass on the narrow road when his companion suddenly shouted 'Watch out! You'll hit them!' Horner looked to the side of the road and promptly stamped his foot on the brake. Approaching them were three men, and had it not been for Horner's quick reaction the car would have smashed into them.

The three wore long cloaks, high riding boots and wide brimmed hats. Their hair was unusually long for the 1930s. They seemed oblivious to the fact that they had almost been run down and continued walking towards the car. Horner and Wright jumped out of the car to talk to the men. But the three men suddenly vanished! The travellers scratched their heads in astonishment, for there was no cover nearby in which the strange men could have hidden. There appears to be only one explanation. Judging from the description of the three men and their dress it would seem that they were probably cavaliers who had been killed in that famous battle almost three hundred years before.

Many ghosts are said to haunt the Tower of London, which is not surprising when you consider the long and sad history of the people who have been imprisoned or executed there. Anne Boleyn has been seen several times, and many people claim to have heard Guy Fawkes wailing through the centuries. Sir Walter Raleigh can sometimes be seen walking the ramparts and Henry VI haunts the chapel in Wakefield Tower.

A most unusual occurrence was experienced at the Tower by Edmund Lenthal Swifte, Keeper of the Crown Jewels, in October 1817. He later wrote an account of the experience:

'I was at supper with my wife, our little boy and my wife's sister in the sitting room of the Jewel House, which is said to have been the "doleful prison" of Anne Boleyn and of the ten bishops whom Oliver Cromwell piously accommodated there. The doors were all closed, heavy and dark curtains were let down over the windows, and the only light in the room was that of two candles on the table. I sat at the foot of the table, my son on my right, my wife fronting the chimney piece and her sister on the opposite side. I had offered a glass of wine and water to my wife, but, in putting it to her lips she paused and exclaimed: "Good God! What is that?" '

'I looked up and saw a cylindrical figure, like a glass tube, something about the thickness of my arm, and hovering between the ceiling and table. Its contents appeared to be a dense fluid, white and pale azure, like to the gathering of a summer cloud, and incessantly rolling and mingling within the cylinder. This lasted about two minutes when it began to move before my sister-in-law, following the oblong shape of the table, before my son and myself. Passing behind my wife it paused for a moment over her right shoulder (observe there was no mirror opposite in which she could then behold it). Instantly she crouched down and with both hands covering her shoulder shrieked out: "Oh Christ! It has seized me!" '

'Even now as I write I feel the horror of that moment. I caught up my chair, striking at the "appearance" with a blow that hit the wainscot behind her. It then crossed the upper end of the table and disappeared in the recess of the opposite window.'

Whatever the object was, Mr. Swifte's action must have scared it off for it was never seen again.

Possibly the most famous ghosts in Britain are

those that haunted Borley Rector in Essex. In 1900 the three daughters of the Reverend Harry Bull, who was the local rector, saw a black nun gliding across the lawn. The nun was not the only ghost to haunt the house. There was also a mysterious girl in white, a ghostly coach and horses that had been seen galloping along roads nearby, headless men and the traditional strange noises within the house itself.

It is said that the principal ghost was that of a French nun. She had been persuaded to leave her convent and to marry the owner of Borley Rectory. According to the story he later strangled his young bride and buried her in the cellar, in the year 1667. No one paid much attention to this story until 1945 when the cellar was dug up. Just one metre below the surface there was discovered the skull of a woman. Perhaps the story was true after all?

The famous ghost-hunter Harry Price called Borley Rectory 'the most haunted house in England.' Price first became interested in the house in 1929 when the Reverend G. E. Smith and his wife were living there. Price interviewed the Smiths and local people and established that a great number of people had seen or experienced the various phenomena associated with the house.

A short while after Price began his investigations the Smiths moved out of the house and the Foysters, an elderly rector and his young wife Marianne, moved in. It was then that the ghosts began their activities in earnest. Bells rang, objects were thrown across the room, there were mysterious knockings from the walls, and furniture was moved from place to place. These mysterious activities seemed to centre on Marianne Foyster. Price eventually came to the conclusion that Marianne was herself responsible for most if not all of these strange happenings for they usually occurred to her while she was alone, or to other people when she was not around.

After the Foysters left the house the ghostly activity more or less disappeared, apart from one or two stories of strange figures seen in the grounds from time to time. In 1937, Price himself rented the house and with his team of investigators subjected it to a thorough investigation. Some phenomena were observed during his stay but it is now thought that Price caused much of this activity himself. But when Price left the house in 1938, the ghost stories did not stop. Shortly after, the rectory burned down and this seemed to raise the ghosts once again, for several people reported seeing wispy figures in the flames around the house. In later years shapes were seen at the windows of the gutted shell of the building. Eventually the building was demolished but it remains to this day one of the most famous cases of ghostly activity in the history of psychical research.

Harry Price wrote two books about the hauntings: *The Most Haunted House in England* and *The End of Borley Rectory*. Although there is now considerable doubt about Price's honesty in the reporting of the phenomena they still make interesting reading. In spite of the fact that the house was burned down in 1939 and Harry Price is now dead, reports of strange happenings in the area still come to light from time to time. The nun whose appearance started off the whole investigation is still seen occasionally. Strange footsteps and the sound of an organ being played have been heard from the church which is just across the road from where the rectory once stood.

Quite often children and animals can see ghosts when adults who are present cannot. It may be that the ghost phenomena is in this respect very similar to that of telepathy. In fact telepathy of some sort may be the reason that ghosts are seen in the first place. Ghost sightings also seem to conform to telepathic reasoning because in the majority of cases people who believe in ghosts appear to be more likely to actually see them than people who do not believe.

It may be, therefore, that ghosts are a projection of our imagination, as could be other strange mysteries such as the Loch Ness Monster or the Abominable Snowman. With certain people perhaps these images can actually become so real that other people can also see them. It also seems feasible that these images both in the semi-solid and the solid state can be projected on to ordinary photographic film.

There are in existence many photographs said to be of ghosts. In the majority of cases these are most definitely faked but there are instances in which photographic experts have examined pictures and cannot find any evidence of faking. It is, however, something that is easy to do. The easiest way to fake a ghost picture, and one that you can try for yourself, is to use a double exposure.

Put the camera on a tripod and get a friend to stand in front of it. If you can get him or her to dress up in a sheet, a monk's cowl, or something similar, so much the better. When you have taken the photograph ask your friend to move away. Continue the exposure of the same scene without your friend in view. When the picture is developed you will have a classic ghost photograph. The ghost of your friend will be visible but you will be able to see through him – just like a traditional ghost!

Denizen of the Deep

The first person to see the Loch Ness Monster was Saint Columba in the 6th century. The saint was standing on the shore of the Scottish loch when he saw a man who had been attacked by the creature. The creature had the cheek to appear for a second time whereupon Saint Columba ordered it to go away. And it did!

Since that time thousands of people have reported seeing the head and neck, the humps, or even just the wake of some unknown amphibious creature swimming in the Loch. The monster remains a mystery, however, for it is very elusive. And although there are an enormous number of sightings recorded, the total number is quite small when one considers the popularity of the area as a holiday resort, the number of curious visitors who go to Loch Ness in the hope of seeing the creature, and the millions of man-hours spent by organised searchers vainly scanning the Loch for any sign of movement.

It is understandable that sightings are few and far between, because the Loch is long and deep and remained isolated until a road was built alongside it in 1933. From that time on sightings became more frequent.

The creature has also been seen on land on several occasions. In September 1913, Margaret Cameron, a teenager, was playing with her sister and her two brothers in the small bay at Inchnacardoch when they heard a noise in the trees. And then they saw it on the far side of the bay. An enormous animal came crashing through the bushes and walked down to the beach. 'It had a huge body, about six feet high and twenty feet long, what we saw of it,' said Margaret. 'It was the colour of an elephant and under it were two big front legs.'

The children were naturally frightened and ran home. But their grandfather, to whom they related their adventure, said that 'it was the Devil that had been after us and we weren't to tell a living soul about it, and so we were put to bed with a big dose of castor oil.'

On 22nd July, 1933, George Spicer and his wife were driving alongside the Loch when they saw the body of a huge animal crossing the road only sixty metres away from them. They estimated the creature to be about a metre and a half in height and anything up to nine metres in length.

A little under six months later the monster was again on land. On this occasion it was spotted by a veterinary student, Arthur Grant, who was riding his motor-cycle. It was one o'clock in the morning and the road ahead was bathed in brilliant moonlight when he saw the creature. It walked across the road and dived into the murky waters of the Loch. When he got home he drew a picture of what he had seen. His drawing shows a large creature

71

with a long neck and tail. In relation to its body the head is very small and the creature has flippers which made its journey across land rather awkward.

The first man to photograph the Loch Ness phenomenon was Hugh Gray, who lived in the area. He saw the monster on 12th November, 1933, and had the presence of mind to take out his box camera and photograph the creature. He took five pictures, but unfortunately only one of them came out.

One month later, on 12th December, 1933, Malcolm Irvine of Scottish Film Productions waited on the bank opposite Urquhart Castle. Eventually his patience was rewarded, for he captured the monster on film for the first time. As with subsequent films there is a great deal of controversy as to exactly what has been photographed. It shows an object sailing along the surface at about nine miles per hour. Many people have said that the object on the film is a log. If this was the case it would be quite remarkable, as logs do not normally travel across water at speed!

Kenneth Wilson, a London surgeon, was gazing at the Loch one day in April, 1934, when something surfaced sixty to ninety metres from the shore. Wilson photographed the object. The picture he took, possibly the most famous photograph of the monster, shows what could be the long neck and small head of a creature.

In addition to the numerous sightings, the large number of photographs and several films of the phenomenon, there is other scientific evidence that something exists in the Loch. On 2nd December, 1954, the drifter *Rival III* was entering the Loch from the Caledonian Canal when the echo sounder picked up something in the water. The resultant picture produced by the sounder indicates that there was a creature some fifteen metres long in the water at a depth of 145 metres. Other experiments with sonar equipment have come up with similar results.

Since 1934, when Sir Edward Mountain had twenty men equipped with cameras and binoculars keeping an eye on the Loch, there have been several organised attempts to solve the mystery. Most of them have been rather disappointing in their results.

Possibly the most successful expedition so far was that of Dr. Robert Rines and his colleagues from the Boston Academy of Applied Science. This expedition's best results came in November 1975, when it was announced they had taken photographs of the creature. To get the photographs, the team used a special electronic flash positioned fourteen metres beneath the surface. But because of the murky conditions within the Loch the pictures were not very clear and had to be improved by a computer.

As could be expected, the photographs brought a barrage of protests from disbelievers. Sir Frank Claringbull, Director of the British Museum, said: 'Five of our experts have seen the pictures of the so-called monster and they do not believe it is an animal. It is a piece of tree.'

It is possible, of course, that such creatures are created in the mind of the observer. People under hypnosis can be made to see things that are not there. Whilst it is not suggested that the witnesses to monster sightings are having us on, it is possible that the power of suggestion plus the power of the mind could work together to create something that appears to be real. Of course this does not explain away the many photographs that have been published said to be of the monsters concerned. It seems incredible to suggest that the power of the mind could produce something so solid it could be captured on film. But why not? Scientists all over the world are examining people who can apparently cause images to appear on film and others who can make inanimate objects move – just by willing it. It is a well established fact that human beings utilise only one tenth of their potential brain power. If we began to use the remaining nine tenths, just think what may become possible – the Loch Ness Monster may become a reality!

In the chapter on the Abominable Snowman and indeed elsewhere in this book, it has been suggested that many strange creatures, including the Loch Ness Monster, might be little more than the creation of our own imaginings. Ernest Jones, a psychoanalyst, wrote of such creatures: 'The simple fact that these animals, in spite of their frequent objectionable behaviour, surprise us by displaying peculiar human characteristics should provide a hint to their real meaning. This is no more and no less than that they represent particular human beings, most often the parents . . .'

In the early 1930s, when the monster sightings were at their peak, the Aquarium Keeper at London Zoo expressed his opinion: 'The case of the monster in Loch Ness is worthy of our attention if only because it presents a striking example of mass hallucination. Any person with the slightest knowledge of human weakness should find no difficulty in understanding how the animal, once having been said to have been seen by a few persons, should shortly afterwards have revealed itself to many more.'

Dr. Maurice Burton, an expert on prehistoric animals at the Natural History Museum for thirty years, stated that: 'All the evidence so far, in my opinion, consists of mistaken observations, hoaxes and poor photographs. The best sightings over the past forty years tie up closely indeed with no more than a family of otters swimming in line.'

Dr. Gordon Sheals, keeper of zoology at the Natural History Museum, has been quoted as saying: 'I find it very difficult to accept that we have a population of large prehistorical reptiles in Loch Ness. One major objection is the complete lack of tangible evidence. Not a single bone has been found. I think we should look for explanations of the sightings in atmosphere and hydrological terms. This monster business is a terrible time-waster.'

When the photographs taken by Dr. Rines' team were published, the British naturalist Sir Peter Scott was reported as being convinced that several of the creatures existed in the Loch. 'I would say there are between twenty and fifty down there,' he said. 'I believe they are related to the plesiosaurs and there is probably a colony of them.'

Dr. Rines and Sir Peter Scott are so convinced that the monster exists that they even went so far as to give it a Latin name in common with all other known creatures. They called it *Nessiteras Rhombopteryx* which means 'the Ness Monster with a diamond shaped fin.' Disbelievers were quick to have a go at that as well. It was not long before someone pointed out that the name is an anagram of 'Monster hoax by Sir Peter S.'

One question that worries a lot of people is: if, as now seems plausible, there are creatures in the Loch, how did they get there? The usual explanation is that the Loch was once part of the sea. Many thousands of years ago the sea flooded the land which enabled sea life to swim into the now submerged Loch. About twelve thousand years ago the sea level fell and the land level began to rise. Eventually the creatures who had stayed within the sheltered waters of the Loch with its abundance of food were trapped in the Loch. Gradually the waters changed from salt to fresh and the creatures also had to change along with their environment. As the Loch was in a remote part of Scotland and difficult to visit, those creatures have been allowed to live undisturbed until the present day.

If, as the evidence seems to suggest, there is not one but several unknown creatures living in the Loch, why is it that the sightings have not been more spectacular? And why have no physical remains been found to prove the creature's existence? If you take a look at the Loch on a map you will begin to appreciate some of the difficulties facing the investigators. The Loch is $22\frac{1}{2}$ miles long, over a mile wide in places and some 230 metres deep. In such an area the monsters become quite insignificant in size. And as, presumably, they are constantly on the move it is little wonder that no-one has yet had a really good look at one.

Some people also believe that there are hidden caves around the edges of the Loch which would help to conceal the creature if it wished to remain unseen.

The Loch is fed by several rivers and streams which bring sediment from local soil. As this is composed mainly of peat it has made the waters of the Loch extremely cloudy. By the time a diver or a camera is only fifteen metres down, the visibility is cut to less than three metres.

It is thought that no physical remains have been found simply because the monsters when they die sink to the bottom of the Loch where their bodies eventually decompose leaving no trace.

The only physical remains of such a creature to be found was a carcass washed up on the beach at Girvan, in Scotland. The creature was about ten and a half metres long and it had a long giraffe-like neck. Unfortunately the locals found the smell of the decaying carcass so revolting they poured oil over it and burnt it!

As this strange creature had obviously lived in the sea it is unlikely that it was the same as 'Nessie'.

Reports of sea monsters are surprisingly common and the seas of the world are so vast it is quite likely forms of life exist in them that are unknown to science.

Power of the Pyramids

The Great Pyramid of Cheops is unique among the Egyptian pyramids and even today, some 5,000 years after its construction, scientists have not managed to unravel all its strange secrets. It is the largest of the pyramids covering a ground area of over thirteen acres. At one time many fantastic claims were made regarding the pyramid. It was said that it stood at the exact centre of the Earth's land mass; that the measurements of the chambers within the pyramids could be used to predict the future; and that the perimeter measurement was connected with the length of the year. All of these ideas have since been proved to be incorrect.

On the other hand people that don't believe the special attributes of the pyramid are quick to point out that it is merely a tomb. They explain away the fact that no body has yet been found in the structure due to the plundering carried out during the first entry made into the pyramid by Abdullah Al Mamun in A.D. 820. But even this does not fit all the facts as we now know them. There is no evidence that any plundering took place although the fact remains that the sarcophagus* is empty: it would seem that either it was never intended as a tomb or that the body of the pharaoh lies somewhere else in a chamber as yet undiscovered. One theory is that the pyramid was intended as some form of astronomical observatory. It is also said that the priests of the time allowed Cheops to think he would be buried in the structure so the pharaoh would provide finance for the great venture.

As a result of the mysteries that surround it the Great Pyramid remains the subject of much speculation. In recent years it has been suggested that the pyramid, and even models of it, possesses remarkable powers.

These powers are said to have first come to light when a Frenchman, Emile Bovis, found several dead rats in one of the central chambers of the Great Pyramid. The thing that surprised him was that the animals had not decayed but were completely preserved. From this discovery the Frenchman began to build up the theory that the shape of the pyramid was responsible for this mummification and for the fact that the bodies of the pharaohs in the tombs had remained mummified for many hundreds of years.

On returning to France he built scale models of the great pyramid. When he put a dead animal inside one of his models it did not decay but became mummified, just like the ones he had found in Egypt. He tried several other experiments but his results were largely ignored until 1957 when Karel Drbal, a Czechoslovakian radio engineer, decided

*The sarcophagus is a stone coffin.

to try similar tests. One of his first attempts was to put a razor blade inside the model pyramid. It remained sharp!

Such is the almost universal belief in the power of the pyramid that it is even possible to buy models of it. It is said that, providing the model pyramid is lined up to the magnetic north, food placed within it never decays, razor blades stay forever sharp, and young plants bloom to maturity faster than normal. It is also claimed that young children allowed to play beneath larger versions of the pyramid remain extremely happy with their environment and that adults who wear a pyramid-shaped 'hat' will find it easier to think clearly and reach important decisions much more readily. Some people have tried sleeping under model pyramids and have found that their dreams are much more vivid and more easily remembered than usual. And when they woke up they said they were much more alert and responsive.

You can make your own pyramid and try some experiments for yourself. The model you make must, however, be accurately made or the experiment will not be successful. It does not matter what size you make your pyramid, but it must conform to the following proportions:

For each centimetre in height the base should have 1.5708 centimetres and the side measurements should have 1.4945 centimetres. Thus if you wish to construct a pyramid ten centimetres high the base measurements will be 15.71 centimetres and the side measurements will be 14.95 centimetres. For a pyramid twenty centimetres high these figures will have to be doubled, and so on.

It is important that each side of the pyramid should be facing one of the four points of the compass. It is, therefore, worth making a stable base on which to place the structure to avoid it being knocked out of alignment. To assist you in putting things into your pyramid without moving it from this essential position make one of the sides of the pyramid into a door by taping it along one edge only.

For best results it is said that any object placed in the pyramid should be placed in the centre and about one third up from the base. To do this you will have to make a small pedestal that is exactly one third of the height of your pyramid. Objects placed on this pedestal directly beneath the point of the pyramid will then be in the same position as the King's Chamber in the Pyramid of Cheops. It is also important that any object placed within the pyramid should be positioned so that its longest dimension is on the line from north to south. You must also keep your pyramid well away from any electrical devices, a difficult thing in most modern houses, or the electrical current will cause the experiments to fail.

If you make a pyramid and also try the dowsing experiments described on page 96 you can try the two together, for it is said that a divining rod or pendulum will react when brought near a model pyramid.

Dreaming of the Future

In the church of Saints Peter and Paul at Swaffham in Norfolk there are wooden statuettes of John Chapman, his wife and dog. They are there because John Chapman put up the money to build the north aisle of the great church. Nothing mysterious in that you may think, but John Chapman was a simple pedlar. How did this simple tradesman come by enough money to finance the building of the aisle? The answer lies in a dream.

One night the pedlar had a strange dream that told him to make his way to London. If he stood on London Bridge he would meet a man who would bring him a great deal of good fortune. The dream was so compelling that John had to go to London to find out if the dream was true. 'You must be crazy!' shouted his wife as he started off on his long walk. 'Taking that much notice of a silly dream!'

After a walk of almost a hundred miles, John eventually arrived in London and made his way to London Bridge. But there was no man there. The people of London were hurrying about their own business and paid no attention to the tired untidy man. For the next three days and through-out the next three nights John kept his vigil. But still no-one approached him. 'My wife was right,' he said to himself. 'Fancy a grown man walking all the way to London just because of a dream!' He was about to set off back home when a man approached him.

'Excuse me,' said the stranger. 'But I keep a shop here on the bridge and I have noticed you standing here for the past three days. I am curious to know why.' So John told the shopkeeper of the dream he had had and how he now expected to be scolded by his wife when he returned home. 'I'm not surprised,' laughed the man. 'Why, if I took notice of dreams I would be in the Norfolk town of Swaffham now, for I dreamt that a man there called John Chapman has a tree in his garden at the base of which is buried a pot of gold!'

When John Chapman returned to Swaffham he decided to dig at the place mentioned in the shopkeeper's dream. Sure enough, there beneath the tree in his garden he found the gold!

In 1779, Lord Thomas Lyttleton had a dream that foretold his death. He dreamed that he saw a woman dressed in white who held in her hand a dead robin. The woman told him to prepare for death as he had only a short time to live. 'Can you tell me how long I am for this world?' asked the frightened man, whereupon the lady in white replied: 'Three days. And you will depart on the hour of twelve.'

The following morning Lord Lyttleton told some of his friends of his dream which, try as he might, he could not forget. They laughed and said he must have drunk too much wine the night before. They explained that his conscience had been disturbed by the fact that he had killed a robin only the previous day.

During the next three days he experienced periods of extreme pleasure followed by bouts of increasing gloom as the fatal hour approached. After dining with his friends during the evening of the third day, he became more and more anxious as the night wore on. Towards midnight he took leave of his guests and went to his bedroom where he and his valet sat looking at his watch as the time of his predicted death approached.

Sweat poured from his brow and he felt a clammy sickness as the final minute went by. Thirty seconds to go. Now twenty, now ten. Then five, four, three, two, one . . . midnight . . . but nothing happened! A few seconds later one of his guests came into the room to see how he was and was surprised to find him in the highest of spirits. 'Ha!' he cried. 'I knew there was nothing to worry about. I have cheated that lady in white. It will take more than a mere dream to kill me off!'

After chatting for a while the guest returned downstairs to relate the good news to the others. Meanwhile the valet was sent off to get his lordship's nightly dose of medicine. When the valet returned he was startled to find his master lying on the bed gasping for breath. He fled downstairs to get help and shortly after the guests rushed into the room. But it was too late. Lord Lyttleton was dead.

'Well, his dream was almost right,' said one. 'But his lady in white got the time wrong. It is now half past twelve.'

Then the valet spoke: 'No, sir. It is not. As the lordship was so upset by his dream I took the liberty earlier today of putting his watch and all the clocks in the house half an hour fast. It is now midnight, so the dream was true.'

Many prophetic dreams are like that of Lord Lyttleton in that they foretell of death or disaster. One of the most famous was that of John Williams of Redruth in Cornwall. On the night of 3rd May, 1812, he dreamt that he visited the House of Commons in London where he saw a man shot. The dream was so vivid, he could even tell that the assassin was wearing a dark green coat with shiny brass buttons. When, in his dream, he asked the name of the dead man, he was told it was the Prime Minister.

He immediately woke up his wife to tell her of the strange dream but she was more interested in sleep. The following day he told his wife again of the dream and during the day he told several of his friends. He thought that he ought to go to London and warn the Prime Minister but his friends only laughed and told him not to worry.

Seven nights after the dream, the Prime Minister, Spencer Perceval, had the very same one! On the morning of 11th May, he, too, told his family. They were worried and tried to stop him attending parliament that day, but Perceval insisted that he had to be present.

Later that day Perceval was walking through

the lobby of the House of Commons when a man stepped out from behind a pillar and shot him. That man was wearing a green coat with shining brass buttons exactly as had been predicted in the dreams of at least two people!

In 1968, Miss Eliot Bliss, a member of the Society for Psychical Research, dreamt she was trying to hide in a city that was being invaded by a hostile force using tanks. She believed that this dream was trying to tell her something that would happen in the future, so she related it to two friends, just in case anything happened. And happen it did – just two weeks later Czechoslovakia was invaded by Russia. As she watched on the television news the tanks rumbling into Prague Miss Bliss recognised several of the places shown although she had never visited the city herself.

The dreams mentioned in this chapter are just a few of the many hundreds that have been recorded. Dreams that have apparently prophecied future events are so common it would seem that they undoubtedly exist. It may be that even more dreams are of this nature. The trouble is of course that accounts of dreams are very seldom written down. So why not try recording your dreams to see if any of them come true? Keep a dream diary and each morning write in it the details of the dream or dreams you had the night before. You never know you may find that some of your dreams have the uncanny habit of coming true.

Triangle of Mystery

There is a mystery in an area just off Bermuda. Aircraft and ships that venture into this strange region are liable to disappear without trace. It is an enigma that has puzzled people for many years and, according to most reports, no satisfactory answer has been found to explain the mysteries of the so-called Bermuda Triangle.

The triangle is an area of about 450,000 square miles of open sea in the Atlantic. The points of the triangle are Bermuda, Puerto Rico, and Miami. It is said that over thirty ships or aeroplanes carrying over a thousand people have vanished in this area. So many stories are told of strange occurrences in this area that it is now almost impossible to separate fact from fiction. But the stories do at least make fascinating reading.

On 5th December, 1945, five TBM Avenger torpedo bombers were on a routine patrol flight from their base at Fort Lauderdale in Florida when the control tower received a frantic message from the flight leader, Lieutenant Charles Taylor. 'Calling tower. Calling tower. This is an emergency. We seem to be off course. There's no land in sight. Repeat. This is an emergency.'

The radio operator in the control tower asked

the lieutenant to give the patrol's position. 'That's just the point,' came the worried voice of the lieutenant. 'We do not know our position.'

This reply puzzled the men in the control tower. Flying conditions were ideal so how could five bombers be lost? Desperately they tried to seek a solution to the dilemma and radioed instructions to the patrol. 'We suggest you bear due west,' they suggested.

'But we don't know which way is west,' replied Taylor. 'Everything seems very strange. Even the sea below us looks extremely unusual! Something is very wrong.'

A little later the voice of one of the other pilots came over the control tower radio: 'Calling control. Calling control. We seem to be completely lost, but we estimate our position to be about 225 miles northeast of base. It looks as if we are . . . ' and the transmission came suddenly to an end. That was the last message to be received from the bombers.

But the control tower operatives were not worried although there seemed to be no reason for the mysterious messages they had received. Each bomber was manned by an experienced crew and every man was trained in survival techniques. Nevertheless a rescue plane, a Martin Mariner flying boat equipped with full survival equipment, was immediately sent out to search for the bombers. At first the rescue operation seemed to be going according to plan but then the flying boat stopped transmitting and was never heard of again.

Later other rescue planes and a number of ships were sent out to search the area for survivors. Although these craft did return safely to their bases they found no signs of the missing aeroplanes. When the American Naval Board carried out an investigation into the affair they could not come up with a satisfactory explanation for the disappearance.

In spite of the reputation which the Bermuda Triangle has, there are many people who have had hair-raising experiences in the area but who have lived to tell the tale. One such survivor was an American bomber in December 1944. In a letter written after the event one of the crew wrote down what happened:

'Not more than three hundred miles from Bermuda on a beautiful clear night, we were suddenly whipped over on our backs, found ourselves on the ceiling one moment and pinned down the next, as the ship was thrown about at an incredible speed. Our pilot was a 240-pound strong man; and our co-pilot was six feet one, and two hundred pounds of hard muscle. I watched them pulling at the wheels with all their combined strength to avert a sure crash into the ocean, only a few hundred feet below. They miraculously pulled out of the dive so close to the water that the wind-generated whitecaps were clearly visible. The entire incident took only a few seconds, perhaps less than one minute, but when we surveyed the crew, eleven frightened men had been reduced to quivering boys who unanimously agreed to resign from the Air Force.'

When they returned to their base they found that only two out of the seven bombers on the mission had arrived safely. All the others had vanished without trace.

Many other strange things have been seen within the triangle. There have been several recorded instances where the final messages have mentioned that the craft was heading into some form of white mist or glowing fog. On occasions vessels have been seen entering these fogs but not reappearing on the other side. At other times people who have entered one of these curious clouds have experienced a 'bending' of time. On one occasion a passenger aeroplane that went into one of these mysterious mists disappeared for a period of ten minutes. During this time the aeroplane vanished completely from radar screens. Afterwards the craft landed quite normally but it was found that all of the clocks and watches on board were ten minutes slow! It appears that time had somehow stopped while they were in the cloud.

There also seem to be an unusual number of UFO sightings in the area. Numerous reports of strange lights in the sky and of glowing craft entering and coming out of the sea have been recorded. One of the first to record this type of phenomena was the explorer Christopher Columbus in October, 1492. He saw a glowing ball of fire that circled his flagship and dived into the sea.

Professor Wayne Meshejian, a physicist at Longwood College, Virginia, engaged in the plotting of weather satellites, noticed that their transmissions were frequently interrupted. This

happened only when the satellite was above the area of the Bermuda Triangle. He thought the reason for this disturbance was the existence of some form of encrgy source beneath the sea which affected the instruments on the satellites.

The theory that there is some unknown magnetic force in the area has been put forward by several people. It has often been noted that the instruments of ships sailing through the triangle go haywire, and that the same thing happened to instruments on board aeroplanes that have flown through the triangle.

According to the experts who have made a study of the Bermuda Triangle mystery there are definitely more craft vanishing under mysterious circumstances in this area than in any other part of the world. Possibly there *is* a magnetic force as yet unknown to man. Perhaps one day the mystery will be solved once and for all.

The Strange Secret of Dowsing

'Dowsing' is a technique used for discovering water, metals, and other objects underground. Traditionally the dowser uses a forked twig of hazel, although other types of branch can also be used. Each hand holds one end of the fork and the dowser then walks over the ground to be surveyed. When he reaches the point above the object he seeks, the twig becomes imbued with a life of its own and moves downward to point at the spot.

Dowsing is a very ancient art but it is said that almost anyone may possess this strange power. Why not try it for yourself to see if you can detect hidden objects in this way?

There are several different ways you can try. To the purists the dowsing, or divining, rod must be of hazel but other woods such as blackthorn, willow or cherry are said to work equally well. Hold each end of the forked section loosely in your fists with the thumbs on top or between the thumb and forefinger of each hand. Alternatively you can try a simple device consisting of two pieces of wire each bent into an L shape. The end of each wire goes into a cotton reel, an old ball point pen, or something similar. It does not matter what you use as long as the wires are free to move from side to side. The holders are held, one in each hand with the wire pointing directly forward. An even simpler device consists of a weight attached to a piece of string. This is held between the finger and thumb of one hand with the weight hanging down.

Now for the test. Place a glass of water on a table and then stand a distance away from it with your dowsing rod or pendulum in your hand. Move slowly towards the water. If you have the power the divining rod will soon tell you. If you use a twig it will move of its own accord down towards the water; the wire rods will move one way or the other; and the pendulum will swing back and forth or round in a circle.

If you are successful with this experiment you can go on to try locating tumblers of water that someone has hidden. Similar experiments can be tried with metal objects, but have a sample of the metal to be found in one hand to concentrate the psychic forces at work. Apparently this is not necessary with water because there is sufficient water in the human body to do this.

Another experiment you can try if you find that you possess this strange ability is to move the divining rod over a map and see how it reacts. It is said that the ability to detect water is so strong that the rod will react over the map above areas of sea, or even over lakes and rivers.

If you find these experiments do not work for you, it is natural that you will not believe such things are possible. But a lot of people claim such powers do exist and there is ample proof to support the idea. American doctors have used divining rods successfully to locate disease in the body; mountain rescuers have used them to locate bodies in the snow; and the American army has used them for detecting land mines. It is amazing what becomes possible when you believe!

Phantoms of the Sea

In 1923, at least four people on a liner sailing from Australia to England saw a strange sight - a sailing ship. Nothing strange about that you may say - until you hear how one of the witnesses described the sight they saw as they sailed near Capetown:

'We looked through binoculars and the ship's telescope, and made out what appeared to be the hull of a sailing ship, luminous; with two distinct masts carrying bare yards, also luminous; no sails were visible, but there was a luminous haze between the masts. There were no navigation lights, and she appeared to be coming closer to us and at the same speed as ourselves. When first sighted she was about three miles away, and when within about half a mile of us she suddenly disappeared ... I shall never forget the second officer's startled expression - "My God, Stone, it's a ghost ship!"'

Such phantoms of the sea have been seen quite often - ever since man first set sail to venture beyond his own lands. But the most well known of all the ghost ships is the legendary *Flying Dutchman*. This famous phantom haunts the seas around the Cape of Good Hope. It is said that the ghostly ship brings doom and disaster to all who see it.

According to legend it is the vessel of Captain Vanderdecken who is doomed to sail the seas forever in punishment for the wickedness of his life. Vanderdecken had a reputation for cruelty but his crew suffered in silence until the day he ordered them to sail around Cape Horn in a violent storm. The sailors protested. 'T'would be madness to round the Horn in such rough weather!' they said. 'Let's lay to until the storm is over.' But Vanderdecken remained adamant. 'Do as I say, you scurvy dogs!' he yelled above the noise of the gale. 'The first man to disobey my order will be thrown overboard to feed the fishes.'

Reluctantly the men steered the courageous little ship into the teeth of the gale. Waves crashed against the bows and washed over the decks; the wind beat ferociously against anything that stood in its path, and everything on board had to be lashed down or it would have been swept overboard. Suddenly the wind caught the sails with such force they were torn from the rigging. 'It's no good, Captain,' they cried. 'We're done for if we continue like this!' In response to their desperate pleas the captain kept his word and threw the crew leader overboard. His cries for help could not be heard above the roar of the wind and for anyone to attempt to save him would have been madness. The crew returned to their duties but as they did so the main mast snapped and crashed down on to the deck.

As soon as the body of the doomed seaman hit the water a flash of light engulfed the ship.

An eerie glowing light, with no discernable shape, materialised near Captain Vanderdecken. 'Abandon this folly,' commanded the light. 'Return to port and you may save what is left of your ship and your crew.' The men fell to their knees in terror but Vanderdecken just laughed. He removed his pistol from his belt and fired at the glowing form. The gun exploded in his hand as the voice boomed: 'Henceforth you shall be forever accursed, condemned to sail an eternal sea until the Day of Judgement. Gall shall be your drink and red hot iron your meat. Of your crew only your cabin boy will remain with you. Horns shall grow out of his head and he shall have the muzzle of a tiger and a skin rougher than a dog-fish.

'And since it is your delight to torment sailors, you shall torment them forever. You will become the evil spirit of the sea and your ship will bring doom and disaster to all who sight it.'

Many seamen have been credited with being the true-life Captain Vanderdecken. The most prominent is Bartholomew Diaz, a Portuguese navigator and explorer. He disappeared in a storm on 29 May, 1500. Another name put forward as the possible source of the legend was the disappearance of the Dutch mariner Bernard Fokke in the 17th century. Fokke had reinforced the masts of his ship with iron to enable him to carry more sail than was usual. As a result he managed to complete journeys much faster than his contemporaries. To the superstitious seamen of the time this uncanny speed was ample proof that Fokke was in league with the Devil, a belief that grew even stronger when the mariner disappeared.

There are several reports of the *Flying Dutchman* being sighted by other vessels. One of the best authenticated is that of the crew of H.M.S. *Severn*. On 6 April, 1821, the captain and crew saw what they thought to be H.M.S. *Barracouta*, another vessel from the same squadron. By the next day the other vessel had vanished and it was later discovered that the *Barracouta* was three hundred miles away at the time of the sighting.

Another ghost ship is sometimes seen off the coast of Rhode Island. This is said to be the ghost of the Dutch vessel, the *Palatine*. In the winter of 1752 the vessel set sail for Philadelphia. On board were a number of Dutch immigrants who wished to settle in America. The voyage was marked by numerous storms which increased in intensity as the vessel neared the American coast.

At this time the captain disappears from the story and it is thought that he was probably murdered by his own crew. Certainly the crew made the most of the situation. They robbed the passengers of all their possessions and then took to the lifeboats, leaving the unfortunate immigrants and the *Palatine* to the mercies of the sea.

Just after Christmas the ship went aground on Block Island, a desolate stretch of land about sixteen kilometres from the coast of Rhode Island. Local fishermen rescued the passengers but one old and demented woman refused to leave the ship. Later the fishermen set light to the ship and it floated off at the next tide with the mad woman screaming from the blazing deck. As the vessel went down all the fishermen believed that would be the last they would see of it. But there they were wrong, for exactly a year later a ghostly ship ablaze from stem to stern was sighted in the area and it has been seen several times since.

One possible explanation for many of these ghostly ships is hallucinations brought on by endless days looking at an empty sea. Sailing, particularly in days gone by, is a lonely life and a hard one. It is quite possible that some of the recorded sightings were brought about by a combination of tiredness, boredom, and frustration.

Many of the ghost ships are seen in misty conditions so it may be that some of them are merely reflections of the vessel on which the observer is standing. Mountaineers are quite familiar with the phenomenon known as 'the Brocken Spectre' which is visible in some parts of the world. The ghost appears as the large figure of a man but all it is in reality is a shadow of the observer cast by a low sun on to a wall of mist. Perhaps some of the phantom ships could have been caused by a similar trick of nature?

A third explanation is simply that of a mirage. Although usually associated with desert areas mirages are quite common at sea. It is quite possible that superstitious sailors could attribute the images they see in a mirage as being phantoms of the sea.

Visitors From Outer Space?

Early in 1979 newspapers all over the world reported the strange sighting of a mystery object flying over New Zealand. The object, a bright pulsating light with three orange rings, was seen by several people and even filmed by a television crew. Similar sightings had been reported over Italy only a short while previously.

Immediately a great deal of speculation was aroused as to what could have caused the phenomena. Scientists, naturally sceptical of anything that cannot be explained by natural causes, suggested that the object was everything from aeroplanes to freak atmospheric conditions, weather balloons, and the planet Venus. But to many people all over the world the sightings proved something they had believed for many years – that our world is being watched by alien beings from outer space.

Ever since Biblical times men have reported seeing strange lights and objects in the sky. There are several instances in the Bible of lights and brilliant chariots racing across the heavens. Ezekiel describes one of these craft that landed near the Chebar River in Chaldea.

In 218 B.C. there were a number of reports of mysterious things in the sky. There are several illustrations of a similar happening over Nuremburg in 1561. During the Second World War aeroplane pilots saw so many unusual lights following their craft that they gave them a special name, 'foo fighters'. At the time both the British and the German pilots assumed the lights were caused by a secret weapon operated by the other side. We now know that neither side had such a weapon and no-one has managed to explain what the pilots saw.

These sightings are now known by the term U.F.O.s, or unidentified flying objects. A more common name is perhaps 'flying saucer' although this description does not necessarily cover every type of mysterious object that has been seen. Modern sightings, and certainly the term 'flying saucer', can be said to date from 1947. An American businessman, Kenneth Arnold, was flying a private plane when he saw nine flat discs 'like piepans and reflecting the sun like a mirror' about twenty-five miles away from him. The objects were flying around mountain peaks near Mount Rainier, Washington, in a most erratic fashion. The official explanation was that the objects were only 'grindstone' clouds. These are flat as Arnold described but, as many people were quick to point out, clouds do not normally fly around!

Arnold's report started a wave of interest, reports, and photographs that has lasted to the present day and shows no signs of letting up. Every

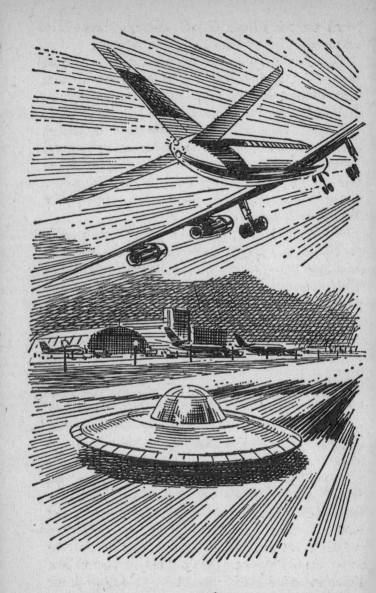

week there is a fresh U.F.O. sighting somewhere in the world.

Some sightings have been witnessed by several people. On 22 December, 1962, a strange circular craft landed on the runway at Buenos Aires airport. A DC-8 jet that was about to land had to take evasive action to avoid hitting the craft. As airport cars and fire engines raced towards it the mysterious craft took off and within a few short seconds had completely disappeared from view. No-one has yet come forward with a satisfactory explanation for the occurrence.

Another sighting witnessed by several people occurred near Dunoon, Scotland in September, 1959. Henry English and his wife, who were holidaying at a nearby caravan site, were driving in their car one evening when they saw two teenage girls at the roadside waving frantically. Mr. English stopped the car and got out, whereupon one of the girls asked: 'Can you see anything up there?'

He looked up and saw two round objects floating in the sky. They made him feel rather scared, but he was convinced that they were real and not caused by a hallucination or a mirage. 'I'd swear they were flying saucers,' he said afterwards.

Later the two girls, Patricia Murchison and Linda McCulloch, described how they had gone for a walk and had sighted the objects on their way home. 'We were walking along the road when we suddenly noticed the two things in the sky. We were scared. We ran into a field at Ardnadam Farm and tried to hide. But they came down until they were just above the telegraph poles. We got up and moved but they followed. We were terrified. We ran into a ditch to hide and they hovered above us. We tried to stop cars on the road but none would stop.'

The girls described the objects they saw as being 'black and white and round, and tapering to a point at the bottom', a description very similar to ones given by other U.F.O. witnesses. When interviewed by the police the officer in charge said he was convinced that the girls were telling the truth about the incident.

Whilst the large majority of so-called U.F.O. sightings can be readily explained away as natural phenomena, misconceptions, faulty observation, and pure hoax there remain a great number of instances where no logical explanation has been forthcoming. With the sightings that cannot be explained simply there is, according to U.F.O. believers, a reluctance on the part of government and military officials to allow the full facts to become known to the public. It is said that some people who have seen U.F.O.s have received mysterious telephone calls from unknown individuals instructing them not to reveal what they saw. If this is true, what could be the reason? Perhaps the officials concerned are frightened there will be mass panic if the real truth were known?

It is, of course, natural that politicians do not want to put the world into a panic by stating that there are such things as flying saucers. So they usually put up some sort of logical explanation for the phenomena. These explanations vary quite considerably and it is said that some are so far fetched they could not possibly be true. It would certainly seem that there is some evidence of an official clamp down on information where certain sightings are concerned.

When all the explanations are sifted and those that are plausible are discarded there are still a lot of sightings that are difficult to explain in natural terms. It may be that some of these are due to natural causes that we do not yet fully understand. There is, for example, a phenomena called 'ball lightning'. Reports of this mention balls of light that move erratically, follow people and objects, and seem to have a will of their own. It could be that many of the so-called flying saucers are really something of this nature.

Another explanation, proposed by some people, is that U.F.O.s are really signs from the Devil – or even the Devil himself. The Reverend Anthony Millican, a Bristol vicar, once saw a U.F.O. and was convinced that it had evil powers. He was out for a walk with his wife when 'we saw a brilliant light on the ground about a hundred yards away. It was like a magnesium flare. As we watched it grew to about the size of a double decker bus. It was a perfectly symmetrical dome shape. Then it became a sort of transparent dirty yellow colour. Up the centre was a black pillar and it hovered about six feet off the ground. We watched, rooted to the spot, for about twenty seconds before it veered slightly to one side and then simply vanished.

'There was an evil feeling coming from it, and there was no doubt in our minds that what we saw was a psychic phenomenon and not a spaceship. For the Christian there is only one creation that can appear and disappear like that. The nearest thing is God's ministering spirits, the angels who can under certain circumstances make themselves visible to man. But we must remember that creation has sinned. There are fallen angels who have the same powers and can appear in any form they choose.'

If flying saucers exist in reality and really are craft from another world, where do they come from? Reports from people who claim to have communicated with the aliens, and have sometimes flown in their craft, tend to disagree as to their origins. One of the most famous contacts was made by George Adamski in America in 1952. He stated that the spaceman he saw told him, through telepathy, that he had come from Venus. Two years later Cedric Allingham met another flying saucer occupant in Scotland. This one indicated by signs and drawings that he had come from Mars. As far as is known life of any sort cannot exist on either of these two planets so it is perhaps possible that the aliens really come from much further afield.

If this is the case the distances to be covered would be so great that the craft would have to travel faster than the speed of light (186,000 miles a second). This would make them invisible which seems to tie in with some of the reports of saucers disappearing in a matter of seconds. Human scientists have no idea of how such a craft could be constructed. But let us suppose for a second or two that such a craft is feasible and that aliens on some dim and distant world have managed to overcome the problem and build such craft. Even then it would take them several hundred years to make the journey to Earth. It hardly seems worth their while, does it? Surely, having made such a journey the contacts they made with us would be much more positive than those that have been reported so far?

It has been suggested by psychologists that people see U.F.O.s because they want to see them. There seems to be some sort of mass hysteria within the human framework that has a need for these strange occurrences. The infinite power of the mind brings them into being – much the same sort of explanation that has been given for some of the other strange things included in this book.

THE END

If you enjoyed this Knight Book you may like to read

THE SPACE EXPLORER'S GALAXY GUIDE

Take a star-studded voyage of discovery with this amazing handbook of facts and fun!

Features include:
JOURNEY TO THE STARS
an action-packed space game to make and play.

SPOT THE PLANET
a clever trick for identifying the various constellations.

UFO SIGHTINGS
WEIRD AND WONDERFUL
MYSTERIES OF SPACE

MAKE YOUR OWN MOONBASE, ROCKETS AND SPACE SUIT

KNIGHT BOOKS